American Accent

Dominika Wrozynski

Winner of the 2017 Sinclair Poetry Prize

Evening Street Press

Sacramento, CA

Evening Street Press

Sacramento, CA

Library of Congress Control Number: 2018950752

Cover: Lu Vickers

ISBN: 978-1-937347-48-2

Printed in the United States of America

10 9 8 7 6 5 4 3 2 1

First Edition

Evening Street Press
2881 Wright Street
Sacramento, CA 95821
www.eveningstreetpress.com

For Helena Krausz and Todd Dorris,
with all my love

TABLE OF CONTENTS

IV.

V.

I.

Spending The Night, Once Again, In My Mother's House

When she sleeps, I trace the remains
of my mother's severed arm. My fingers
invade the fleshy canyon where the stitches

once held together nightmares of scalpels
and too little ether. Her veins are estuaries—
all lead to a maw of silence. It twitches once

and I know she is embarrassed, even in sleep,
that the arm still moves—tries to burrow into
itself like an apple snail, surprised at its own

exposure. The nerve synapses never cease
firing, searching for missing blood. She does
not desire the attention. Why unveil something

she has hidden behind silk shawls and stuffed
into trench coat sleeves? This is why she'll only let
me see it at night—because she knows I am

the missing half, as if the doctor clove us in two
and never asked permission. Tonight I will try
to find my way back, try to fit my cells into hers again.

My Mother's Biography

Because you ask me to write your biography
I start with the humble caramel and rose
georgette you wear to the courthouse
when you marry my father, how your
witnesses forget that you are missing
an arm, have been missing it for years.
You announce your first-born will be a girl.

But you want me to start with the *Uni*
in Kraków—how you never finish psychology
because communist profs ask trick questions
you refuse to answer. Or perhaps when you are
ten and the teacher's book leaves a crescent scar
on your cheek bone—so close to your retina
you realize then that you can always lose

the language for *światło*—the light that stays
on at night in your room. You want me
to know *miłość*, the comet's tail you tape
to my ceiling, and *wolność*—the fireworks
of your first Fourth. So when you write a novel
on breaks at the candy factory, I know you will
never leave me a will. You send me CDs of your radio

show—all Polish, all the time—and I drown
in the hard *d's* and *cz's*, feel the burn of the *r*
drawing a thin line across my throat. But your
tongue comforts with sibilant *smoki, jaskółki, sosny.*
I inherit the language that fills your kitchen,
syllables that escape parted lips while you sleep,
the language in which the priest will christen my children.

Poland, 1945

Your three-year-old arm, white as rain-soaked
birch, dangles above your mother's kitchen

linoleum. They'll have to cut it, you know,
sever the elastic marrow: cells, dervishes

without a trajectory, will never duplicate.
You will wake in your own bed—goose feathers

that make you sneeze—missing the German
Shepherd you let escape from the gate, rub

the raised scar on your ankle where he bit
down. When it thunders, the absent arm

will tell secrets you already know are dripping
down orange-shingled roofs: the Nazi soldier

who discharged the rifle was really your older
brother, for the first time wielding a gun,

not a paintbrush: you will pose—a sulfur butterfly
pinned to the canvas of living room walls by his bullet.

And though he will be sorry—paint you from the neck
up—you will still dream of pirouetting solo across an empty stage.

The Things We Take

The night is hoot owls, wind-whistled flue, babies bundled in burlap.
—Judy Jordan

This night is a single marigold backpack, and a gray
faux-fur coat, and a doll that says *Mama* when you flip

her over, a doll that could cost us everything. And this
night is also three suitcases, one for each of us, the three

bears, but no Goldilocks to try things out first, only friends
who stay up all night and pray rosary upon rosary, wrapping

us in bandages of Hail Marys and Our Fathers, in an invisibility
cloak of luck and Polish superstition. This night is English

dictionaries wedged into one suitcase, and American dollars
stuffed into the bottoms of socks, and three changes of clothes

each, and no children's books. The single book will come later,
when we are on a three-day Christmas cruise to Germany.

It's the most expensive thing in the gift shop, but we buy it
anyway, spend the dollars. It's a good investment—the child

teaches herself to read and the mother is not angry about white
tights, the fall upon the boardwalk. This night is always what stays:

bags slashed open, other fathers stalled in political purgatory, one
girl's jumper missing in the school's morning roll call. This night

is finally the customs agent who tells us to go through, even though
the doll is hollow, still says *Mama*, and we are never coming back.

Mama Makes *Pierogi*

When power lines drag heavy clouds,
cold comes and Mama makes *pierogi*,
rolls out dough with old beer bottles,

tries not to think about when she was a Mrs.
She slices dough with a tailor's precision.
Scraps fall like cloth shards, weightless

until they thunk onto the cutting board,
remind her she creates dinner for two,
not three. Her daughter sneaks around

the kitchen door. Fingers, floured hummingbirds,
trap meat and cabbage, pinch pinch pinch
the pockets closed. She stands for hours

on kitchen tiles, compounds her vertebrae
into question marks. Her daughter, underfoot,
receives a dusting of flour. Bubbles burst

the water in the steel pot, and Mama drops
in *pierogi*, steams up the windows. Her daughter
draws tulips upon each pane, waits for winter

to pass. Years later, the daughter, not yet a mother,
makes gummy *pierogi* that fall apart in stew pots,
sends cabbage and gray meat floating to the top.

Our America

for my father
"America I've given you all and now I'm nothing."—Allen Ginsberg

You came home late, smelling of Meat Supremes
and hand-tossed crusts. I was nine and drowned

in your red jacket when I delivered pizza to stuffed
animals. They always tipped well. You brought me

promo toys—rubber dragons and slippery bats
wrapped in plastic—that should have been kept away

from children. Most nights, before you fell asleep—
half-smoked Camel in the ashtray, Leonard Cohen

on the tape deck, Heineken warming by the television—
you'd tell me everything we would one day have

in our America. But your list didn't include the white
Renault that never started in snow, or the white Toyota

that you sold me years later that left me stranded
on Sunday, on the freeway, when all of the tow truck

drivers had gone to church. It didn't include a landlord
with a mail order bride and a howling Teacup Poodle,

or his daughter who ate only sugar cubes in her training
to become an Olympic gymnast. You forgot the hot days,

made even hotter by asphalt you laid, a smell you never
washed out completely—and the Cocker Spaniel

we rescued together, the same dog I watched die after you
left. So when I watch you sleep and know, by your eyelids,

that you are dreaming, I wonder whether your list includes
owning your own theater, or whether it has to include

the refinishing business where you will always restore other
people's antiques. I doubt the kidney stone that sent you

to the emergency room is on this list, and you have probably
left off the pen that you give me for Christmas, every year

that we speak, and the refills I can never find after the ink
runs out. Does the list include the death of your father,

and a funeral held in another country without you? Maybe
it just includes you drinking the orange vodka you made

in your new kitchen, and a back screen door that slams
shut in the night, though there is no wind.

Dear Johnny Castle

Though we were only nine, and Jasmine was from Turkey,
and I was from Poland, we were suddenly American, too,
and wanted that summer at Kellerman's in the Catskills
to last forever, just like Baby did. We wanted to grow up

faster so we could make mambo magic with you,
and when Penny, your best-friend-ex-Rockette told us
to *shake 'em*, we wanted those maracas to be real, though
they wouldn't be for years. We cheered for the justice of it

all, when you told Robby-the-scumbag-waiter:
You just put your pickle on everybody's plate, college boy,
and leave the hard stuff to me. And when we saw the sign:
STAFF QUARTERS, NO GUESTS PLEASE,

we ignored it, too. We carried that watermelon,
and felt our knees give out when you crooked
your finger and cocked your head, and led us
onto the dance floor for the first time so we could roll

our hips in the wrong direction after you spun us dizzy.
And we knew you were trouble, in the pits of our stomachs,
or maybe lower, and we didn't care that our fathers had
already decided on the kinds of boys we'd marry.

All we wanted to do that entire summer was to dance
the Mashed Potato with you, on that famous log,
though we fell off the balance beam in Jasmine's basement
every couple of steps, and so settled for slow-dancing

with the couch cushions, imagining ourselves
in your cabin, with Otis Redding crooning "Arms of Mine"
on the record player, while we told you: *I'm scared*
of walking out of this room and never feeling, the rest of my life,

the way I feel when I'm with you. And though boyfriends
would never hear this line, we'd whisper it to you every night
before bed, and you would dip us low, and kiss us high
between our shoulder blades, behind our newly-pierced earlobes.

And then we'd always remember that August summer,
when we almost broke the VCR's "rewind" button
watching the final dance number, that summer before
we knew you were the only one who'd ever love us right.

My Mother's Kraków

Rush hour—I ride a bus in Kraków,
the city of my mother's birth, and give
up my seat for an old woman carrying
young potatoes in a red-mesh grocery
sack. She will boil them in the old pot,
sprinkle them with dill, and pour glasses
of buttermilk—bounty as elusive as God
these days. I say *Please take the seat*,
in a Polish tongue awkward from disuse.
She stands, looks past me into smog
outside of the window, the sun hanging
low over the city like a bruised peach.

Trial By Fire

for my mother

I can only think of how you nearly drowned in *duende's*
dark water, after the fire didn't burn you or your brother's

paintings, your silhouette seared onto the window
frame. You cannot sleep nights, you tell me, fear

the flames' lick of your hair. And you don't fear much.
This is nothing after communist Poland. All you wanted

was to never disappear down the side door to an interrogation
cellar. But there *is* something, after all, about the end

punctuation of a burned house. That dark water forces
you to give all of your candles to Goodwill, only allows

for three hours of sleep at night. And when the glass
of milk, brandy, or the walk before bed all fail, I will

string St. Barbara medallions around your bed, hide them
behind the vanity, under the cat's collar. I want a guarantee

from the nun in the cathedral gift shop that this is the best
saint for the job. I will go to Goodwill and get your candles back.

My Mother Receives Her Citizenship

Yes, I will bear arms in defense of my country.
My mother, fifty-two, five-foot-two, has never

held a gun. Her eyes flash shell shock when police
pepper protestors downtown, remind her

of communist Poland, where guns performed
interrogations in concrete cells. Citizenship

waned through bruised craniums and busted ribs.
Now it is desired. My mother is ready to bear arms

with one arm, the other shot away by a German soldier
during World War II. Another unwanted Polka:

an impostor in the country of his birth. Today she pledges
allegiance to a foreign flag, says *yes* to impossible questions.

Sparring with the One-Armed *Pierogi* Maker

When you are stung by wasps, I have to admit
     I first think about your arm, so white when you came
to Florida to visit, and smooth now, so swollen
     by the stings that you feel young again, the veins far
below the surface where no one can find them.

The baking soda brings down the swelling,
     but the wasps have marked you, stained your skin.
You stuck your arm right into their nest,
     didn't recognize the cardboard incubator on your balcony.
When they swarmed you, I was two thousand

miles away. I am sorry when you visited
     we fought—it had been a while since we made each other cry,
but this visit we stung and stung. And then you
     left and stuck your arm in that nest. If you were allergic,
that might have been it. I refuse the *it* now,

instead imagine you a wasp warrior, landing
     a back flip before punting the nest onto the neighbor's
balcony. This is the way the One-Armed *Pierogi* Maker—
     the only superhero I ever believed in—takes care of business.
I miss you even more when, the very next day,

I don't see the wasp nest on the underside
     of my cannas lily leaf, when my face is just far enough away,
when they sting my hand instead. I am grateful
     for the instant swelling, and the stain that won't leave—
like the birthmark on my left calf, the birthmark

you say I have because, when you were pregnant,
     you saw a rat in an apartment hallway in Poland and slapped
your leg, thinking only of protecting the potential
     of me. You marked me then as your own, but now I am always
quicker to anger, more unsure about forgiveness,

and louder than you—especially in my laughter.
     Everyone who meets us, though, sees the same do-it-yourself
remedies, cotton balls that fill our ears to avoid drafts,
     our recipe-free cooking, the same superstitions—how we refuse
to hold each other across a threshold for fear our love will fly out the door.

II.

Desert Love Poem

This is our second Christmas, the make-it-or-break-it
Christmas where we decide. I didn't know whether
I would still love you tomorrow. So today you've left
on a hunt for a natural tree because we are both tired
of talking and my mother is coming to spend her first
Christmas in New Mexico, eat green chile rice at your
parents', get to know their Chihuahuas as the dogs
hump her leg. I wanted her to have a tree, not from
the Walmart parking lot, but a pine from the mesa,
cut by you with a blunt axe—the only one we have.
You will refuse to wear gloves, knick your thumb, swear
into the year's first snow. But you will bring it back,
remember when you hunted trees with your father last
year, how his beard caught the sudden storm, and how
he dragged the prize through his asthma home to your
mother. She cried that night, cursed him for almost
killing you both. You will then understand how she
leaned into your father after she was tired of talking,
after there was nothing more to say.

Patrick Swayze in New Mexico: Star Sightings You Don't Write Home About

He hunkers in plaid shirts now, hides lips that made women
swoon behind year-old stubble, spins the corner bar stool
at The Hitching Post, the rancher dive that only serves Bud.

The El Fidel and Joe's Ringside have 86ed him already, joined
his name to the list of honorable mentions, like the brothers
who fought pit bulls behind the Immaculate Conception

Church. But this is Las Vegas, New Mexico, city of Billy the Kid,
and Doc Holiday's Saloon. Roosevelt's Roughriders remain
dusty knickknacks in an adobe museum, open only

on Wednesdays. Here the devil says goodnight, at the base
of the Sangre de Cristos, where Jesus would have run out
of water and loaves, would have to settle for iced tea

and hot tortillas made daily at the Spic n' Span Diner,
once a laundromat. No matter what he did, Jesus could
never be *from here*. Patrick, too, is only humored

by the bartender because she remembers ingesting
electricity, tonguing his face on the television screen.
So when we see him, we want to throw him a doughnut,

a rope, a life raft, dress him in black Carhart, waterproof him
for the coming monsoon season. It is what happens to children
whose parents have grown old. We fear his passing. But above

all else we want to shift his beer belly into the center
and surround him with college co-eds, because we are all
better than to let Patrick Swayze drink alone in a corner.

Cock Fight
Tijeras, NM

Among the desert paintbrush, you are the rattler
your father warned you about. Belly rakes across
dirt and with every one of your boy muscles
you feel the drought in the earth. It's the heat

that's made everyone crazy. You smell the blood
before you see it, like heat lightning that never
makes it to earth, the stillborn barn kitten you
buried, your father's scrubs after an all-night

shift at the VA hospital. And you hear the roosters
growling—low, not like Laverne and Shirley, the pigs
you heard at slaughter when your parents thought
you were too far away. You know the whipping

that will come later. But you must see them. Must see
what you imagine will spill out of the *gallodrome*, feathers
sticky and sparse, clotted blood on each cockspur.
The formula is just out of your reach now, the secret

alchemy of language the roosters hear before they fight.
You are the caretaker of strays—too many dogs and cats—
though they somehow still fit into the trailer on the mountain.
But sometimes you forget to feed them, relegated

to your room hungry. Your parents believe in examples.
That's why you have to see these roosters, because they
are just like the chickens in the backyard—but someone
has failed them, as you failed all of the animals the night

you left them hungry, when you rode bikes with the neighbor
boys until dark. You wonder if you have that power,
too, if you can turn instinct on its head and make
the cats rip off each other's ears, whiskers.

Patrick Swayze at the Albuquerque Balloon Fiesta

It's the first time he's ever seen the Glow and it's not yet dawn, and Patrick's
      been waiting in line since 2:00 a.m., still wishing
for the star treatment. But it's worth it, as the balloon envelopes light up,
      propane burners breathing together, baskets

in a disciplined row. One by one, they rise into the sky, like a kickline
      of showgirls he once saw in Vegas—their sequins
bright as supernovas in the dark theater. This is really where he likes
      to watch the balloons—on the ground. He can't

imagine dangling from a gondola, on invisible thermals that could bring
      it all down. And the height—impossible. Patrick recalls
how much trouble he had on that log in *Dirty Dancing*—they almost gave
      the part to Harry Connick Jr. But after sunrise,

and well into his fourth Bloody Mary, Patrick decides that today is the day
      he, too, will rise, and look down, and stop being afraid.
He will call the director of *Jump: The Musical* and tell him skydiving is no longer
      a problem. Patrick finally settles on a harvest-colored

beauty piloted by Eddie Clemens, ballooning's notorious bad boy, though Patrick
      doesn't know this as he climbs aboard, knuckling the ropes
so tightly he feels them chafing patterns into his palms. What follows is contentious—
      Eddie broadcasts over the CB that he hates nervous passengers

after he tests the gondola's safety by rocking it back and forth hundreds of feet up.
      Patrick can only look straight out, instead of down,
which incenses Eddie and makes him forget how to pilot the balloon. Or maybe
      the truth lies closer to the shifting wind—though Eddie

will claim that his foolproof spit test established the wind's direction. But he hasn't
      refueled all day, so now the gondola is drifting low
over the interstate and Patrick knows the balloon has to land somewhere.
      He begins to understand why Louis XVI ordered

criminals to be the first to pilot hot air balloons—if something went wrong,
      who would miss them? But people would miss
Patrick Swayze. Not just those internet fans who still hold *Road House* viewing
      marathons every month, name their mulleted sons

Dalton, and drive Buick Rivieras, either—real fans who know he writes poetry
and records acoustic guitar music when no one is looking.
Patrick prays through Eddie's cussing and though "Death by Hot-Air Balloon"
would have given him *The Enquirer*'s front page, today

continues in obscurity as Eddie maneuvers over the interstate and lands in someone's
back yard. Children surround the gondola, clamor for trading
cards. But even now, after narrowly avoiding demise by power lines, Eddie announces
he puts all of his money into the balloon, not into trading cards.

This is where Patrick draws the line. These may be future fans—and you never turn away
fans. So in a moment inspired by the thin air Patrick tried
to inhale while in flight, he offers the children signed head shots—glossies he carries
for situations such as these. And even though most of them

will throw the head shots in the nearest arroyo, and Patrick's face will mingle
with pizza boxes and float in-between used diapers until
the next time the rains come, a few will take the pictures home, tell their parents
of the day they saw Patrick Swayze fall out of the sky.

The Hillcrest Hotel and Diner

Las Vegas, New Mexico

Five months from Halloween, the waitress bobs between tables
in silver garland halo and wings. She could be an outpatient—
there are two hospitals in this tiny town, both mental, and a university

no one remembers. "Red or green, *mi'jita?*" she asks. I don't speak
Spanish, don't want her to think I'll listen to her long day or admire
snapshots of her kids, mariachis with pint-sized guitars and sequined

smiles. But I know my allusions, my symbols. Red is hot, so I choose
green, but in one bite know green chile means liquid fire in New Mexico,
and I am hungry now, no symbol necessary for a *gringa* out of water.

Now I still punctuate sentences with "*Que no?*" and miss the chile —
necessary as salt. I wonder whether Ben, my favorite schizophrenic,
has ceased scaring students working late in the library stacks,

and whether he's found a computer where the vampire voices
have fallen silent. I hope the Hillcrest still serves the chicken fried
steak. I write letters to the haloed waitress, dog-ear *mi'jita* in the dictionary.

Train Accident: Austin, Texas

The reigning Miss Deaf Texas died Monday afternoon after being struck by a train.
A witness told Austin television station KTBC the train sounded its horn right up
until the accident occurred.

But what of the driver who sounded the horn, heralding
an entire choir of premature angels? Does he worship
at the roadside shrine, tend the *descanso* and slow the train

every time he comes around the curve, just a little, so the candles
won't blow out, though they do every time? Does he remember
his throat jamming, his teeth screaming, the gears locking,

his eyes closing when he knew she would not turn around?
Can he ever forget her hair, piled high, Texas-style, or her
jacket—as small as a doll's? Did he ever put his ear

on the tracks when he was young, feel the tremolo
as it came nearer? And when he finds her silver ID bracelet
soldered to the track, does he press his fingers into the worry

quarter he carries in his pocket, the very first quarter
he ever put in the path of an oncoming train? How hot
the metal after the train had forged it, how soft.

Wake at Don Kiyote Books & Ephemera

for M. Carroll (Las Vegas, New Mexico)

It's a night for skin walkers, I think, as we mourn
you in the only way we know how, sitting around

a used bookstore, theorizing grief. We deny that
anti-depressants plus prostate cancer make for an attic

hanging. But they do, you argue. They do.
Do your remember when I fell asleep during Kant?

You were the only one who knew that I had been
at the hot springs just outside of town last night, watching

teenagers make out, wishing I could disappear into the desert,
into that which could only be the Sublime. You became

a shadow of yourself—Vega said your aura was green—
I thought maybe she wasn't making it up this time—

you were already going, deconstructing your kidneys,
your prostate, until all that was left was your skin,

translucent around your temples, veins diverting
blood away from the heart. But the skin is replaceable.

Though at what price, ask the Navajo. What are you going
to give for a dark resurrection, comical on any other day?

Except I dreamt you last night, riding your bike to class
with one pant leg up—black sweats, wool beanie. But you

never arrived—rode the same streets, waited for the same light.
What can it hurt, to come back as a coyote hunched

on the university bell tower, and lick the bell's tongue?
What can it hurt to test the strength of the cornmeal

that circles our beds, keeping you at bay? What will you give,
Sweet Atheist, now that your soul is safely erased from the equation?

Patrick Swayze Waits In Line To See Jesus

Not in a warm tortilla, the butter slowly absorbed
by the furrows in Jesus' forehead. He has five of those,
shellacked and framed, hung in the den next to the Big

Mouth Billy Bass. To Patrick, Jesus on a tortilla has become
old hat. But this is the first morning the horses' water trough
has iced over, and not finding salvation in the ice crystals,

he leaves his ranch, finds a line in front of the stop sign
on 6th Street. Here the faithful wait, orderly, for a glimpse
of the Savior. He's on the stop sign, reports the news anchor.

The frost—look into the frost. And they are looking, and taking
pictures, this strange dawn queue of old farmers, business
owners, college students. The children race in-between legs,
shouting, "We're gonna see Jesus!" Patrick's not so sure.

Everyone gets to see Jesus? Maybe it's like the entrance bar
in amusement parks—maybe you have to be a certain height
to see Jesus. No one under four feet allowed. But maybe

height has nothing to do with it. What if Jesus will only
appear if you bring him an offering? What could he give?
He does have a few hundred extra acres of land he wouldn't miss—

Jesus could have those. He'll even throw in horses—the old
Arabian and the slow Paint could go. A fishing rod for the trout
pond, too—he's always taken Jesus for the fishing type.

So when it's his turn, Patrick stares at his pristine cowboy
boots, and finally raises his eyes to meet *his*. Only, Jesus
is no longer accepting applications—he's melted.

Now Patrick has no proof, again, that he ever was. He guesses
that's what they mean about faith—how you have to believe
in these stop sign miracles, melted Jesus and all.

Winterizing

The world takes a day off its calendar, and spins
haphazardly—a child's mobile, no start or finish.
The first snow of the year covers out-of-the-way
New Mexico towns, while flakes cover your lashes
as you start the car before it's time to go. You calm
the cats. They fear the wind that tears at shingles,
destroys winter gardens. Cocoa appears by my bed,
where I huddle into spring. Finally you are able
to show off your prowess in all things outdoors.
Hiking boots track in salt from our walkways.
The pipes won't freeze. We'll never run out of wood.

III.

The Story of Our House

For me, the rogue centipede in our bed
        is the beginning because, for the first time, I am

brave enough to kill one. But maybe
        I should start with the family of pileated woodpeckers

I watched from our newly washed kitchen
        window, when you were at work. They dug in the silver

oak carcass across the yard, red heads diving
        into dead wood. Will you ever believe me—about them—

because they've never returned? And now
        I am like those ornithologists who spent years chasing

the Ivory-billed, willing it back from extinction
        into myth. You might want the story to begin with our

never-ending search for barred owls
        in the backyard, how we build shrines of binoculars

and flashlights in every room, how we wait
        for dusk. Just when we've let our minds tally the cost

of tonight's dinner, their calls startle us back
        into our hunter-selves, the soft hooting turning into

a phonograph needle skipping and scraping
        against the vinyl of treetops. Maybe the squirrels, too fat

on acorns, are our daily beginnings, kept alive
        on birdseed we buy in bulk and goodwill. And when we walk

across the sponge of our front lawn tomorrow,
        we can't forget that the moles and armadillos were in the earth

before us, after all, snug in their darkness,
        unaware of the new animals starting a home above.

Living in Florida, I Have Replaced *Cicada* with *Love Bug*

For September in Florida say *love bug* instead,
because this is the month we fly in opposite

directions in a seasonal tug-of-war. Say *love bug*
for lust because they are undiscerning, and so

we want to be, finally cool in the air we dare call
"crisp," the air we funnel into our bedroom in a tiny,

glorious tornado. For aerial stunt say *love bug*, though
the fliers often kamikaze into forests of manly leg hair,

or ping-pong off our windshields, but continue their furious
mating. For female, too, say *love bug*, or maybe for vixen,

because she is usually larger, forces the male to go where she
wants, finds another if he lets go. Whisper *love bug* for intruders,

their appearance imminent on the inside of the screen door,
though they will not steal anything but our patience, elude

the indoor cats. For scientific fact, say *love bug*, genetic engineering
a creation myth used to explain their origins, their never-ending

numbers, their prompt spring and fall takeover of roads, cities.
Finally, replace silence with *love bug*, because we are forced

to close our mouths while outdoors, for fear they will nest
in our throats—hungry for this season of singing.

Like Linus, In Love

Just when we want to give up, we see him, an old man
        of a pumpkin, beady eyes and a pinched
mouth that droops without the dentures he left at home,
        and a nose to rival Cyrano's. We know

that this is the one, much sooner than I knew this about you,
        in that dive bar where I never learned
to inhale, where you wrestled drunk karaoke stars to the ground,
        and where I was a connoisseur of liquid-fire

liquor and Olympia beer—quality we judged by the can's
        expiration date. So we'll lug Mr. Nose
to the kitchen, where he will stare with eyes that float in sockets
        you will carve so meticulously, just like you

organize your closet, the sock drawer through which I relish
        rummaging. We know that he will win.
And as we watch trick-or-treaters who do not own waterproof
        costumes, I will want to freeze us, make us

into smiling tee-shirts, send us like rebellious satellites past
        the earth's gravitational pull, past Jupiter's
crimson maelstrom and Saturn's rings, even past Pluto's
        long, cold orbit around the sun.

Elegy for Minnie's 24-Hour Café—Closed for Remodeling, Indefinitely

Four a. m. and still we are not finished with our conversation,
currently covering your father, where he's been for decades,

the question almost weightless tonight, sandwiched between
two crackers. We have come from the bar to coffee, no longer

glowing from just the right number of drinks but always hungry.
The food arrives late, but still we eat Brie and fruit because they last

longer than burgers. Your heavy hands swallow grapes that re-emerge
in your mouth like a magician's trick quarters. We argue because I want

to drive you to your job at the drywall plant, watch the sun rise over
the factories in the Industrial District. You'd rather ride your bike,

fly over steep downtown streets, eight miles each way. The waiter ignores
us, has lost all hope of getting paid, but allows us to loiter, even though

the coffee has run out. We finally leave when you have to go shovel the gypsum
that settles deep into your pores. Sometimes they let you drive the forklift.

Years later, we have exhausted each other's fathers, moved on to when you'll be
home, and whether the cats will ever cease eating the plastic we use to seal

windows before the surprise snow. Tonight we hunger for Brie and grapes,
but Minnie's is dark, our booth selling online as a hip piece of history.

Saving the Small Miracles

Temperatures in the 80s make us reconsider
buying a palm tree for Christmas, but we go
to the Boy Scout lot anyway. It's how we pick

everything. The stray cats we own are no exception,
and neither are the dinged dishes, the hand-me-down
flower pots I recycle every spring in the hopes of making

something grow. Perfection be damned, I think, tugging
at the single rose thread in the pashmina I wear to defy
the Florida weather. These weavers got it right, adding

the flaw, the pale thread in a black scarf. I've given up
wrapping the pashmina so it doesn't show, instead want
everyone to look twice, try to pick off the thread, the proverbial

sore thumb now as wondrous as the moon at perigee. Since
for the weavers, God is the only perfection, the only one who
can clean his plate and not leave that single obligatory bite,

they must hide flaws in the cloth, remind us that we once reached,
fell, and hit the ground—hard. So this year I panic when we can't
find a little loser pine, the Boy Scouts older, more intimidating

and business savvy. Gone are the days of the ten dollar miracle.
Our deal this year is a forty dollar cookie-cutter nightmare.
Or so we think, until we drag it into the house and watch it drop

half its needles, the branches too weak for ornaments, too thin
to camouflage the plastic light strands. So while somewhere angels
sing the Baby Jesus into being, we celebrate our bald beauty with shots

of eggnog, red-faced renditions of Santa Baby. The cats bite
each other's necks, lick the flocking off the gold icicles,
and wrestle under the tree skirt, and all is calm and bright.

Drinking Becomes Them

Your mother gigglesnorts newborns. Your father—
love child of Santa Claus and Jerry Garcia—turns

red, redder, twists his way around the room
without music, whispers, "Ugly baby," collapses

into an overstuffed La-Z-Boy, laughing. I'm
not family, but should be, when a cousin spills

mint schnapps on my open-toes. Alcohol stains,
sticks in-between. Someone's son discovers

your father gives freely when drunk. He's already
made twelve dollars and change. Mom fingers

Dad's wallet from his pocket as he fumbles
for another dollar. I want to drink like this

when we're fifty, let children pilfer our open
pockets, dance without music until morning.

IV.

The Days Between

The week begins with a hornet's nest in our stairwell—

the insects large and dangerous, I think,
really dangerous. *But you've got to hand it
to them,* you say, *look at the size of that nest.*

When the first cold snap arrives, I think
they are dead, but then one stretches its wings
and triggers the group, sends it, frenzied, to work.

And it ends with your cousin's death—

though I'll never know, when they find her,
whether her arms are folded or spread wide
in her bed. Wide, I hope, like long, weathered wings.

Your mother calls to instruct you, says you
have to *let down*, and I want to kiss Prince,
because when we blast "Little Red Corvette," you finally do.

Retrieval

The desert has taken you, though right now you lie
in our bed. Your body will not cease its Hanging Man
pose, part of the tarot deck you never learned to read.

In sleep, you are louder than awake, your septum still
deviated, and I wonder how it is that you can really
come back from war. I imagine you return one limb

at a time, one joint. First your legs cease running,
then your toes spread out in sandals you haven't worn
in a year. You stop biting cuticles and allow your hands

to rest on the leather of the steering wheel, on the small
of my back, on the cat's fur. But some things take longer,
and I can't always find the quick wink. Instead there are

tendons I'm afraid will pop like over-strung guitars, sinews
that twitch at the start of a lawnmower. That's when I think
you'll never come back, a nomad lost in shifting dunes.

Record Keeper Of All You Want To Forget

1.
I know there are charred bodies
in those pictures you won't let me see.

I know what it means to investigate,
though not what it means to drive across
the Kuwaiti border in the back of a humvee
with a bull's-eye on its back, with the Kevlar
vest your parents sent you underneath
a starched white shirt.

Your crew cut and khaki pants do not belong
here—Kuwaiti men don't often have red hair.
But the general likes you, soldier, likes the way
you do things,

he says, and presses a coin into your palm—
a general's coin: it smells sterile,

you think, like a surgeon's scalpel. It's an honor,
he says. A heavy honor,

you think. An honor to be given this coin,
he says. An honor to document the dead,

you think, to add new names you make every effort
to pronounce to the list.

And now you are tied forever to these angry,
pale hills dotted with oilrigs—giant clumsy
beetles, burrowing deep into the land.

I'm not surprised when you do show me pictures
of the Kuwaiti skyline—skyscrapers that rival those
in American cities. It's beautiful,
you say, when there are no explosions.

2.

Your lens zooms in on the woman's hair, framing
her face just so, or the bias of a crocheted shawl
that cuts a black swath across her waist. Either way,
you won't focus on her legs, no longer there.

You want to know her name—her Arabic name—
not the translation.

You want to hear the syllables that still belong to her,
want to weave their husky silk into a shroud.

You wonder if your name has a translation,
if you exist in Arabic, if you could have been born
here. You could certainly die here,

you think, and they will write your number
on a metal box, and it will only matter to your parents
then, who will engrave it on prayer cards.

If your commanders ever check these pictures
you never take, this woman will be long gone,
buried by her brother who never wanted to meet
you, who wants you to do your job and get the hell out
of his city, while the smokestacks continue pouring black
clouds, and your nose bleeds at least once a day.

I Will Still Visit

I tell my friend, M., I want her to plan our next trip. She is a master-traveler, and I know this will keep her busy. She needs something to do when a car bomb splits apart Ashrafiyeh, the Beirut neighborhood where her parents live, the neighborhood where she teaches Arabic to Americans every summer— the neighborhood I promised her I'd visit.

M. has lived through enough war.

She cannot enter my cellar because the smell reminds her of hiding in basements with her mother as Israeli planes dropped bombs on Beirut. She knows cockroaches and bodies and thick, days-long darkness. She wears shoes—even now inside her American home—because she is always ready to run.

So when I read reports that tourism in Lebanon will suffer, I tell M. that I will still come. I want to meet her father, tour his clothing shop, watch him invent yet another household gadget that drives his family crazy. I want her mother to make me that squid dish, whose name I do not yet know. And I want to eat so much of it that my mouth becomes black from the ink. On the weekend, I want to go to the family mountain house, too, sit on the balcony and eat green raw almonds and drink cold beer. I want to stay up talking all night and watch the sun rise over the village, over a home not very different from my own.

I've Never Been Anyone's "Old Lady"
WWII Veterans' Parade, Carabelle, FL

Though no one's weekend warrior woman, or hot-hog-accoutrement,
      I don my Darth-Vaderesque helmet and we mount up,
join seagulls and pelicans, flying in formation towards the ocean, wind

battering my non-aerodynamic head, snapping my tailored, non-biker
      leather jacket across my back like a twisted wet towel;
and as we lead a fleet of bikes in the 4-block parade, in this tiny coastal

town, I think that finally I am as settled on the back of your cruiser as I am
      riding shotgun in the car—because, though I hate
to admit it, you are usually the better driver, and by "better" I mean more

aware of secret potholes that I always hit, or the pressure of the brake pedal—
      much harder to gauge in high-heeled boots.
Today, the two vets who still can, walk amidst the 10-foot flags we clutch

next to each motorcycle, and for an hour they are soldiers again. And though
      you are half their age, today you imagine yourself far away
from Florida, storming foreign beaches. I don't salute because I'm afraid

of getting it wrong, but your hand's sharp angle is just right for these
      old-timers, and when we ride across Ochlockonee
Bay that night, the wind wants to send us arcing across the bridge banister

like awkward, leathered birds, but you fight it the whole way, only
      revealing later the odometer hit "666" as we crossed
the middle of the bridge. At home, when I wrestle a comb through my hair,

I understand why the Harley-mamas don't wear helmets, instead binding
      their bleached manes with pink skull-and-crossbones
bandanas; but I'll never give up the helmet, because my brain will be even

more necessary after gravity takes care of my breasts and ass, and I don't
      think you want me to give it up, either, because
you know I'm willing to ride it all out with you, to block the wind at your back.

10-Year Anniversary

The almanac says to buy you something made of metal,

> but you already own those coin cufflinks you never wear,
> and our plastic cocktail shaker works just as well. In this union,
> partnership, anything but a marriage, we've already framed
> leftover license plates—New Mexico's hot air balloons climbing
> up the kitchen wall, Florida's oranges rolling around our basement.

Instead, I want to give you the smell of the ocean

> on the first day of every beach season, and the sun-filtered
> green of oak leaves that shock us into spring. A decade
> is worth more than sundials and birdbaths. It's worth
> the hollering of barred owls in the middle of the night,
> worth the offering of their spotted feathers on our deck.
> It's worth the cross-country moving trucks, sick housecats,
> knowing we will always hear the language of each other's sleep.

My wish for you tonight is flight, for the wind

> to sweep you above our rooftop, above our small green city;
> and though I can't give you wings, I hope the helicopter lesson
> will be a good stand-in; because a decade is worth the shaky
> takeoff and landing, the stories you will tell me of the pint-sized
> farmhouses and wisps of rivers, your birds-eye view above it all.

V.

The Endangered Body, Not Yet Extinct

When my wrists ache from too much untrained typing—
    curled fingers hunting and pecking their way across the keyboard
        like skittering chickens—and when the sudden Florida cold cracks

my skin into raw mosaics, I can hold my own with the best
    complainers I know. These Polish women survived—first the Germans,
        then forty-five years of Russians. They clicked rosary beads together in deep

pockets and kept their mouths shut. Children and husbands
    sat in solitary cells while the women waited for coffee and meat
        in lines as slow as ancient animals, stretching from hours to days.

Now they can finally talk, about nerves or cholesterol—no state
    rations on maladies. An obsession with the heart, and its sudden
        stopping, drives them to funeral homes to pick out casket colors.

Every day brings a new disease, the possibility of one-upping
    the neighbor in the catalog of endangered organs. So it's in my genes
        to find a sunspot that will become melanoma if I worry enough, rather than

ask for help with the recurring headaches, or the depression
    that gnaws the light away from my edges. One morning with only
        the empty house as witness, I fall out of bed, tangled in my comforter

after dreaming disasters all night—intestinal cancer, all of my teeth
    rotting out at once. I pick myself up and know that this is silence
        I must keep. My brain will have to be fine on its own, without

a scan, maybe with a few rosary rounds for good measure,
    complaints saved for the stubbed toe or paper cut. Now if you ask
        why I worry my temples the next day at work, I'll just tell you I slept funny.

Why My Mother and I Only Drink Too Much Once a Year

We even drink whiskey the same, which is not well, I discover,
      calling my mother, with next-day-shame
and gut-rot. She, still a Polish Catholic, because there are no rules
      against drinking and because Mary saves

our collective souls every day, asks, *Did you lose the reel?* by which
      she means, do I remember? And I think I do—
mostly—remember that I drank rye whiskey with men twice my size,
      and I was smarter this night, and the drilling

in my hip bones and knees finally stopped, even though they still
      divined rain. I left my hair down, and no one
knew it had gotten so long. I forget if my mother's hair was down,
      too, on the one day she drank too much and lost

the reel, the day she fell through our frosted bathroom door
      and I finally woke up. We had, earlier that night,
completed our bedtime ritual—I could only sleep clutching her
      pointer finger, amazed every morning she had

freed herself. But there was my mother, fallen through the glass,
      pointer finger shredded, and I knew, even
with stitches, that the finger had lost its mystery. *We do much better
      with clear liquors,* she says. *Vodka will never*

make you lose the reel. And I feel slightly-less-than Polish, because
      I've never taken the 80-proof shot of Żubrówka
to wash down a piece of black, smoked eel—the skin wet leather
      that wedges itself between teeth. The vacation summer

I was fifteen and mortified, in the tiny Polish restaurant, my mother
      tipped back the shot as if it were water, the origin
of its name—said she wished she still smoked slim cigarettes in opera
      holders. Even then I knew that medieval herbalists

were right, proclaiming vodka could "increase fertility and awaken
      lust." Indeed, I thought, watching my mother
extend her pinky as she took another, her hand a swallow sweeping
      circles around the table, and the waiter's eyes

on her like hungry midnight tomcats yowling their desire.
　　　But the reel was not lost that night,
and my mother, the finest weaver, simply spun us all together,
　　　our ragged threads glowing in her fingers.

Upon Seeing the Inside of Your Knee in Pictures
for Todd

We marvel at the whiteness of bone, your patella
two smooth halves of an undiscovered moon,

a black ravine between them where I desperately hope
there is still a fancy Latin-named ligament that holds

everything together. That ravine is where I insert
my contradictions, my fear that your knee will be

our most accurate weatherman. Your lateral meniscus
is so new to us, a strange artifact we were never meant

to see, and when the surgeons realign it, shave the tear
that splits its rim, maybe they will cross the nerves,

or miss one, and instead you will predict the day my soufflé
finally rises, or the hour our old cat calls it quits. You might

think it silly, my love, that I know you've been robbed,
and that I wonder where the torn bit of the meniscus even is,

and whether the rest of your cells miss it, too, now that they
have to go without. But it makes my mouth hurt to look

at your excavated insides. The pockets where my wisdom teeth
once were are tender today, the clove oil I massage into them

only numbing the gums. And I want those teeth back,
want the roots to make me wiser again, though I was

awake when they took them, felt my tired jaw finally
give them up, its bruised hinge opening like a ready valley.

Ode to the Dirt Eaters
For S. and J.

Because you extol the speed in which it is possible to grow
new squash when maggots devour mine last summer—

the blossoms pale, flimsy tissue paper, and because you
avoid every bump in the pavement when you drive me—

clutching my abdomen—to the doctor, and because you rescue
runty cat after runty cat and they become fat guardians

of your duplexes—their Buddha bellies talismans we rub for luck,
and because you recycle toilet paper rolls, use only cloth napkins

and enter a compact, buying nothing new for a year—except
underwear and the occasional cocktail, and because you

"borrow" tiki torches from a sorority and throw me a birthday,
complete with bocce ball, though the balls get lost in the Confederate

Jasmine trellis, and because you spend your anniversary protesting
Big Coal in Kentucky and start a Queer Studies major in an Iowa university,

and because you allow your brother to move in with you,
even though it means giving up cooking the curry you love

and eating meat again, and because you spend your free time
teaching in prisons and last-chance high schools, and because

you smuggle bourbon into a dry county in unmarked cardboard
boxes—just in case friends come to visit—maybe that is why

you never care what I make for dinner, why I know even if I serve
you dirt, the loamy Florida soil spilling sunset over the lips of uneven

ceramic bowls, that you will relish the layers of mushroom
compost, that your tongue will remember the quartz

and feldspar mixing with calcite and gypsum a hundred
years ago, and that we will all be sated once more.

To All of the Poets Who Say, *Don't Write Poems About Your Dog*

What would you have me do, though, when the stray
red hound almost dies in my driveway, when her paws
are so swollen from dehydration and mange that she cannot
walk any farther along our country road,

when she is covered in her own blood from so many fleas
and mosquitos, and when she wheezes every so often
like a seasoned smoker? What should I do
after I feed and water her, after I bathe her skin—

stretched taut against each rib, after I find her redneck
owners who love her so much they don't notice she is gone
for days, after they give her to me because she is just
"too damn smart" for their pathetic fence?

You might say: *Put that dog poem in the drawer.*

But then you'd never know she makes it, that she brings me
a bone every morning, that her tail can only wag—like a boat
propeller—in circles instead of side-to-side. You'd never know
that her heart somersaults around her chest—even when she sleeps—

because a valve never closed just right. I realize you might not
care. But you must know that I don't have another way
to remember what is important, another way to heal, another
small way to make my world right.

My Mother Shops For A Prosthetic Arm

Not out of a catalog—though she wishes she could paper
her bedroom with glossy, two-armed beauties with perfect
fingers, the hands sea stars—sure of their grip, curling

around a target prey. She imagines running ten fingers
through her hair, twisting until pain burrows into her scalp,
rolling each strand onto curlers, finally holding the metal

pin between fingers, not teeth. Instead she misses three
bus connections to the university hospital, meets a resident
who asks about the last time she's had sex. My mother

is in amputee hell—worse than 1945 when she lost her arm.
The doctor, followed by a gaggle of students, is not much
better, asking her to disrobe, probing scar tissue. My mother

is nervous and the stump jumps in the doctor's hands, wants
to make a run for the door. He is thrilled—a modern Dr.
Frankenstein, she thinks. *Five functions, ma'am. Think of five*

dream functions you want your prosthetic to perform. My mother
makes a list that includes driving a stick shift cross-country.
She'd also like to go fishing with the new arm, reel in lake

trout with her father, though he's been dead for thirty years.
And ballet—she wants the new arm to gain her admission
into a conservatory. She wants her partner to raise her

toward the ceiling and she will arc both arms over her
head. At the end of the show she will receive so many
roses that she cannot hold them all. But the doctor

wants her to shake hands, grip railings. She promises
to return for the fitting of her very ordinary arm,
though she knows she's lying as she catches the bus home.

Elegy for William Witherup, Poet

William Witherup, a Seattle poet, playwright and activist, whose work focused on people who lived downwind of the Hanford nuclear reservation, racism and technology, has died. He was 74.

Dear Bill: It's been a few years now—time not important—
      because you are still dead. Yesterday, a student in workshop
asked me what a euphemism was, and was it like saying
      passed away when you really meant *died*. Yes, I said, and knew
that you preferred death to passing away, the blunt finality
      over the gradual untethering. I want you to know that I miss
you—in the most un-poetic of ways: no similes for my sadness.
      When we met, you brought me your poems to that Seattle
bank and I read them in the teller window, quit my job,
      went to grad school. I should have wiped away all of your overdrafts.

The next time I saw you was in New Mexico—you came
      to read at my no-name university, and brought a dead crow
you found outside to the after-party. *We can't waste this*
      beauty, you said. While the host hyperventilated in the corner,
another student cradled the crow—promised you she'd use
      the slick feathers. She said she did. Maybe you knew she didn't—
but you were still happy that night, surrounded by young misfits who loved you.

I didn't know until another poet told me about the obituary:
      Acute myeloid leukemia, which I know you blamed on the Hanford
plant. I blame them, too. First your father, then you—
      cancer linking you like a nuclear ouroboros. You will be 4-years-dead
in 10 days; I do not know this until I begin writing.
      But I think the sudden wind storm today, tearing through my
magnolias, lets me know that you are still rockin' it out
      somewhere in the cosmos, smoking peyote with Ginsberg,
brushing your muse's lusty hair, and walking your dog,
      Non Sequitur, in a never-ending field of light.

The Remarkable Body

When the doctor reads the ultrasound
and tells me I have an *unremarkable gallbladder*,
I laugh, and she must think I'm one of those
hypochondriacs who submit to unnecessary
tests just to hear the good news—and maybe
I am. But when the world is breaking apart,
and I know I can't solder it back together
with my Red Cross donation, I am grateful
for good health, steadfast as my flannel sheets.

I do want to know whether she let her nurses
see my boring gallbladder, and maybe my kidneys,
too—depurating sieves that have never done
anything else. Do they now know the blueprints
I will never see? And what about my uterus—equally
as unremarkable to her when she found out
it had never contained anything but possibility?
During the ultrasound I hold my breath, over
and over, because she has to see around my ribs,

which she could do without, because they block
her view. But I know they are the staunch palace
entryway to the kidneys, the last-hold-out guards
of my heart—which has proven itself remarkable,
and of my spleen—the Pocket-Hercules that wages
war against my old blood cells. And though medicine
tells me it is non-vital, I am grateful for the gallbladder,
too, the secret pear nestled next to my duodenum.
I could go without, but why excise that rainy day nest egg,
the favor from a forgotten reserve that I have never called in?

Lizard Calls to Tell You He is Dying

You think he might actually be right this time.

It wasn't the professional bull riding
that did him in, though he'll lift up
his shirt every time he sees you, just to make
sure you haven't forgotten the spiral scar
swerving along his stomach—extended now
from years of case-of-beer nights and cheeseburgers.

It wasn't driving the skiers around

Crested Butte, either, though the roads are
covered in snow almost year-round
and we marvel at the daily pictures:
the white rooftops mid-May, the thermometer
a permanent twenty degrees.

Lizard will tell you it was the wives—

your mother was his seventh. He's up to
nine now, and we have one theory as to
why this one's lasted so long: she owns a liquor store.

Congestive Heart Failure, says the doctor

when you ask what he really has—that,
and a stubborn streak. Most
people will do anything to live longer. Lizard
just wants to know whether the oxygen tank will
prevent him from smoking cigarettes.
When the doctor tells him to move to a lower altitude,
Lizard flips him the bird and crosses his real name off each medical chart.

I know you are readying yourself for the trip

because dying is the only way he can get you
to visit. You're his physical mirror
image and the other possibilities scare you even
more. But when you see him, don't worry about any of that.

Show him that you haven't forgotten how to ride

the old Paint horse around the frozen
pasture, and that you can still pull back the
string on his compound bow. Light his cigarette,
load up his oxygen tank into the old truck, and drive him
to the top of the Continental Divide. And when you have to stop
for a herd of elk, or maybe mountain goats, don't honk the horn.
Light Lizard another cigarette and watch them walk by.

Everyday Worship

The dogs are on their way and you are bringing them
to me, though you don't think it's a good idea
and you have told me so. The weather in New York
is extraordinary today, and reminds me of the weather
in Iowa, where I watched storms fly across plains. The clouds
were gray dogs, rolling in swathes of sky, all tails and teeth.

Jane and John's farmhouse, where I wait, is lived-in
in all the ways we both love. Stairs are impossibly narrow
and crooked doors don't shut. There is pulled pork
in the slow cooker and a basement with bottles of red wine
for me and beer for you. And there are tiny altars in each room:

a scrap of silk, phlox in a silver vase. My favorite has wisdom
teeth in a sugar bowl where they join a kaleidoscope of river
pebbles. Worship here is every day. And though it is already
deep May and the peonies have opened, my skin still itches
from too much winter and instead of worrying about
whether we will love each other through another season,

I revel in minor disasters like the heat of the coming
summer breathing into my ear while I sleep,
and your cousin who homeschools her children in front of the TV.
And when you arrive with the howling, slobbering parts
of my heart, I have already decided that the dogs will get deer ticks
when they run outside, or that they'll get hit by a car

on the nearby road, or that they'll drown in the swift creek
behind the house. And one of them does get the deer tick,
which you remove with a precision I've never seen. We learn to love
each other just enough at the altar of dogs, and let them off-leash.
They almost run into the road, but they don't, and they swim out
into the creek but always come back to our shore, and we crave
their freedom racing each other across the field, crave their restless
bodies still running deep into their dreams that night.

Salvage

Biking through north Florida woods at the peak of summer,
      we search for blue trail markers, find only the scabby bark

of Southern pines. Never ready for the transition, always
      too scared to carry speed through the turns, I fall when the trail

turns to sand. When it dead-ends in a swamp, I imagine
      that we'll end up on page seven of the local paper after the alligators

leave us, half-eaten, in the mud. And when the yellow flies
      swarm, I drown in wings. They are in my hair, crawling under

my eyelashes, jarring open my lips. How I wish, then,
      for those flies to be kernels of golden grain, and I the boy

in T. R. Hummer's poem, drowning in a silo, my *arms*
      too thin for wings, overwhelmed by love for all that's bright.

Instead, I can't breathe and we are so far from salvation
      that I do not know what to move, where to run, until you swat

my head and arms, yell at me to *Go! Ride!* And I do ride—
      hard—finally fast enough to conquer the sand. When I look

you are not behind me, and I fear the flies have claimed you
      until I see you muscle your mountain bike through the weeds.

As we find the trail, I know you are the only one I want
      with me when we surprise the white-tailed deer, when they allow

us close before they smell our sunscreen. We watch them
      bound away and I know that you saved me today, again,

as a matter of course, and I am no longer afraid of the flies
      or gators, no longer afraid of the sand, of losing my way home.

Acknowledgments

Many, many thanks to the editors and readers of the following journals in which these poems first appeared, sometimes in earlier versions or under different titles:

Belletrist Magazine: "Dear Johnny Castle," "Upon Seeing the Inside of Your Knee in Pictures"

Temenos: "The Story of Our House"

The Tishman Review: "10-Year Anniversary"

New Madrid: Journal of Contemporary Literature: "Everyday Worship," "Lizard Calls to Tell You He is Dying"

Nimrod International Journal of Prose and Poetry: "Drinking Becomes Them"

Balanced Rock: The North Salem Review of Art, Photography and Literature: "The Days Between"

Five Points: A Journal of Literature & Art: "My Mother's Kraków"

The Grief Diaries: "Wake at Don Kiyote Books & Ephemera"

Birmingham Poetry Review: "I Will Still Visit"

Rattle: "Desert Love Poem"

Saw Palm: Florida Literature and Art: "Sparring with the One-Armed *Pierogi* Maker," "Salvage"

Proud to Be: Writing by American Warriors 3: "Retrieval," "Record Keeper of All You Want to Forget"

One Image: One Hundred Voices: "To All of the Poets Who Say, *Don't Write Poems About Your Dog*"

200 New Mexico Poems: "Patrick Swayze in New Mexico: Star Sightings You Don't Write Home About"

The Portland Review: "Living in Florida, I Have Replaced *Cicada* with *Love Bug*," "Cock Fight"

The Spoon River Poetry Review: "My Mother's Biography," "Spending the Night, Once Again, In My Mother's House"

Kritya: A Journal of Poetry: "Mama Makes *Pierogi*," "My Mother Receives Her Citizenship," "Trial By Fire," "The Things We Take"

Slipstream: "My Mother Shops for a Prosthetic Arm"

Crab Orchard Review: "Poland, 1945"

I am grateful for the kindness and generosity of many writers, teachers, and friends. Thank you to David Higginbotham for the tough love—I *am* a better poet than I am a fiction writer.

To my Tallahassee literary community: I am so lucky that I was able to spend almost a decade with you. Thank you for showing me what it means to write fearlessly and how to live my best life.

To my writing group members Sara Pennington, Jennifer Perrine, Jen McClanaghan, Jane Springer, Laura Newton, Deborah Hall, and Christine Poreba: You have been the definitions of ferocity, honesty, and grace. You have kicked my ass, and you have loved me and believed in this book from the beginning. Sarah Grieve, you are the best writing partner/road trip maven/scorpion-killing superhero.

To my writing teachers at Florida State: your generosity is unparalleled. Jimmy Kimbrell, thanks for always suggesting the right edit, the right revision. This book is infinitely stronger for it. David Kirby, thank you for showing me how to tell stories and for always believing that I had some that were worth telling. Barbara Hamby, thank you for your work on this book and for being willing to share your brilliance with me. I am more ambitious, everyday, because of you.

To Lu Vickers: Thank you for creating gorgeous art and for gifting me with your photograph for the cover.

To my Manhattan College colleagues: Thank you for welcoming me into a very special club where you make me a better writer and better teacher.

To my "local" neighbors and friends in Patterson, Brewster, and Carmel, NY, especially Paul, Mina, Julia, Sanna, Zoë, and Cory. You make *home* a reality and not just an idea.

To Mireille, Stacey, and Jameson: Thank you for your love and friendship.

To Evening Street Press and Barbara Bergmann: Thank you for wanting this book and for shepherding it into the world.

To my parents, Henryk Wrozynski and Helena Krausz: You fled communist Poland, leaving behind friends, family, careers, and literally sacrificed everything you had ever known so that I could have a life in America. I am so proud to be an immigrant and to be your daughter.

Finally, to Todd Kayne Dorris: The highs and lows and milestones are one thing. It's the days between that mean the most. This is for you, my love, with endless gratitude for the days between.